Books by Mark Strand

POETRY

The Story of Our Lives, with The Monument, and The Late Hour   2002
Blizzard of One   1998
Dark Harbor   1993
Reasons for Moving, Darker, & The Sargentville Notebook   1992
The Continuous Life   1990
Selected Poems   1980
The Late Hour   1978
The Story of Our Lives   1973, 2002
Darker   1970
Reasons for Moving   1968
Sleeping with One Eye Open   1964

PROSE

The Weather of Words   2000
Mr. and Mrs. Baby   1985
The Monument   1978

TRANSLATIONS

Looking for Poetry   2002
(POEMS BY CARLOS DRUMMOND DE ANDRADE AND RAFAEL ALBERTI)

Travelling in the Family   1986
(POEMS BY CARLOS DRUMMOND DE ANDRADE,
WITH THOMAS COLCHIE)

The Owl's Insomnia   1973
(POEMS BY RAFAEL ALBERTI)

ART BOOKS

Hopper   1993, 2001
William Bailey   1987
Art of the Real   1983

FOR CHILDREN

Rembrandt Takes a Walk   1986
The Night Book   1985
The Planet of Lost Things   1982

ANTHOLOGIES

The Golden Ecco Anthology   1994
The Best American Poetry (WITH DAVID LEHMAN)   1991
Another Republic (WITH CHARLES SIMIC)   1976
New Poetry of Mexico (WITH OCTAVIO PAZ)   1970
The Contemporary American Poets   1969

Blizzard of One

Mark Strand

Blizzard of One

P O E M S

Alfred A. Knopf   New York   2012

THIS IS A BORZOI BOOK
PUBLISHED BY ALFRED A. KNOPF

Library of Congress Cataloging-in-Publication Data

Strand, Mark
Blizzard of one : poems / Mark Strand.
p. cm.
ISBN 0-375-40139-3 / pbk 0-375-70137-0
ISBN 978-0-375-70137-5
I. Title.
PS3569.T69B57   1998   97-49172
811'.54—dc21   CIP

Published June 1, 1998
First Paperback Edition Published February 13, 2000

ACKNOWLEDGMENTS

Thanks to the editors of the following magazines in which some of the poems in this book first appeared:

AGNI REVIEW: *The Next Time*
BOULEVARD: *A Suite of Appearances*
ELM: *Five Dogs (3)*
INDIANA REVIEW: *Five Dogs (1)*
LONDON REVIEW OF BOOKS: *The View*
THE NEW YORKER: *Untitled; The Great Poet Returns; Our Masterpiece is the Private Life; A Piece of the Storm; Here; Some Last Words; In Memory of Joseph Brodsky; Five Dogs (2 and 4)*
OPEN CITY: *Five Dogs (5)*
OXFORD QUARTERLY: *What It Was*
PARTISAN REVIEW: *The Delirium Waltz*
PN REVIEW: *Two De Chiricos*
SLATE: *Precious Little*
TIMES LITERARY SUPPLEMENT: *The Beach Hotel; Old Man Leaves Party; Morning, Noon, and Night*
WESTERN HUMANITIES REVIEW: *I Will Love the Twenty-first Century*

Thanks to the Rockefeller Center at Bellagio for a residency during which some of these poems were written.

FOR TOM & JESSICA

Contents

I

Untitled

As FOR the poem The Adorable One slipped into your pocket,
Which began, "I think continually about us, the superhuman, how
We fly around saying, 'Hi, I'm So-and-So, and who are you?'"
It has been years since you bothered to read it. But now
In this lavender light under the shade of the pines the time
Seems right. The dust of a passion, the dark crumble of images
Down the page are all that remain. And she was beautiful,
And the poem, you thought at the time, was equally so.
The lavender turns to ash. The clouds disappear. Where
Is she now? And where is that boy who stood for hours
Outside her house, learning too late that something is always
About to happen just at the moment it serves no purpose at all?

The Beach Hotel

OH, LOOK, the ship is sailing without us! And the wind
Is from the east, and the next ship leaves in a year.
Let's go back to the beach hotel where the rain never stops,
Where the garden, green and shadow-filled, says, in the rarest
Of whispers, "Beware of encroachment." We can stroll, can visit
The dead decked out in their ashen pajamas, and after a tour
Of the birches, can lie on the rumpled bed, watching
The ancient moonlight creep across the floor. The window panes
Will shake, and waves of darkness, cold, uncalled-for, grim,
Will cover us. And into the close and mirrored catacombs of sleep
We'll fall, and there in the faded light discover the bones,
The dust, the bitter remains of someone who might have been
              Had we not taken his place.

Old Man Leaves Party

It was clear when I left the party
That though I was over eighty I still had
A beautiful body. The moon shone down as it will
On moments of deep introspection. The wind held its breath.
And look, somebody left a mirror leaning against a tree.
Making sure that I was alone, I took off my shirt.
The flowers of bear grass nodded their moonwashed heads.
I took off my pants and the magpies circled the redwoods.
Down in the valley the creaking river was flowing once more.
How strange that I should stand in the wilds alone with my body.
I know what you are thinking. I was like you once. But now
With so much before me, so many emerald trees, and
Weed-whitened fields, mountains and lakes, how could I not
Be only myself, this dream of flesh, from moment to moment?

I Will Love the Twenty-first Century

DINNER was getting cold. The guests, hoping for quick,
Impersonal, random encounters of the usual sort, were sprawled
In the bedrooms. The potatoes were hard, the beans soft, the
    meat—
There was no meat. The winter sun had turned the elms and
    houses yellow;
Deer were moving down the road like refugees; and in the
    driveway, cats
Were warming themselves on the hood of a car. Then a man
    turned
And said to me: "Although I love the past, the dark of it,
The weight of it teaching us nothing, the loss of it, the all
Of it asking for nothing, I will love the twenty-first century more,
For in it I see someone in bathrobe and slippers, brown-eyed and
    poor,
Walking through snow without leaving so much as a footprint
    behind."
            "Oh," I said, putting my hat on, "Oh."

The Next Time

I

NOBODY sees it happening, but the architecture of our time
Is becoming the architecture of the next time. And the dazzle

Of light upon the waters is as nothing beside the changes
Wrought therein, just as our waywardness means

Nothing against the steady pull of things over the edge.
Nobody can stop the flow, but nobody can start it either.

Time slips by; our sorrows do not turn into poems,
And what is invisible stays that way. Desire has fled,

Leaving only a trace of perfume in its wake,
And so many people we loved have gone,

And no voice comes from outer space, from the folds
Of dust and carpets of wind to tell us that this

Is the way it was meant to happen, that if only we knew
How long the ruins would last we would never complain.

The Next Time

II

PERFECTION is out of the question for people like us,
So why plug away at the same old self when the landscape

Has opened its arms and given us marvelous shrines
To flock towards? The great motels to the west are waiting,

In somebody's yard a pristine dog is hoping that we'll drive by,
And on the rubber surface of a lake people bobbing up and down

Will wave. The highway comes right to the door, so let's
Take off before the world out there burns up. Life should be more

Than the body's weight working itself from room to room.
A turn through the forest will do us good, so will a spin

Among the farms. Just think of the chickens strutting,
The cows swinging their udders, and flicking their tails at flies.

And one can imagine prisms of summer light breaking against
The silent, haze-filled sleep of the farmer and his wife.

The Next Time

III

IT COULD have been another story, the one that was meant
Instead of the one that happened. Living like this,

Hoping to revise what has been false or rendered unreadable
Is not what we wanted. Believing that the intended story

Would have been like a day in the west when everything
Is tirelessly present—the mountains casting their long shadow

Over the valley where the wind sings its circular tune
And trees respond with a dry clapping of leaves—was overly

Simple no doubt, and short-sighted. For soon the leaves,
Having gone black, would fall, and the annulling snow

Would pillow the walk, and we, with shovels in hand, would meet,
Bow, and scrape the sidewalk clean. What else would there be

This late in the day for us but desire to make amends
And start again, the sun's compassion as it disappears?

The Night, The Porch

To STARE at nothing is to learn by heart
What all of us will be swept into, and baring oneself
To the wind is feeling the ungraspable somewhere close by.
Trees can sway or be still. Day or night can be what they wish.
What we desire, more than a season or weather, is the comfort
Of being strangers, at least to ourselves. This is the crux
Of the matter, which is why even now we seem to be waiting
For something whose appearance would be its vanishing—
The sound, say, of a few leaves falling, or just one leaf,
Or less. There is no end to what we can learn. The book out there
Tells us as much, and was never written with us in mind.

Precious Little

For Bill and Sandy Bailey

IF BLINDNESS is blind to itself
Then vision will come.
You open the door that was your shield,
And walk out into the coils of wind
And blurred tattoos of light that mar the ground.
The day feels cold on your skin.
"Out of my way," you say to whatever is waiting, "Out of my way."
In a trice the purple thunder draws back, the tulip drops
Its petals, the path is clear.
You head west over the Great
Divide and down through canyons into an endless valley.
The air is pure, the houses are vacant.
Off in the distance the wind—all ice and feeling—
Invents a tree and a harp, and begins to play.
What could be better—long phrases of air stirring the leaves,
The leaves turning? But listen again. Is it really the wind,
Or is it the sound of somebody running
One step ahead of the dark?
And if it is, and nothing turns out
As you thought, then what is the difference
Between blindness lost and blindness regained?

The Great Poet Returns

WHEN THE light poured down through a hole in the clouds,
We knew the great poet was going to show. And he did.
A limousine with all white tires and stained-glass windows
Dropped him off. And then, with a clear and soundless fluency,
He strode into the hall. There was a hush. His wings were big.
The cut of his suit, the width of his tie, were out of date.
When he spoke, the air seemed whitened by imagined cries.
The worm of desire bore into the heart of everyone there.
There were tears in their eyes. The great one was better than ever.
"No need to rush," he said at the close of the reading, "the end
Of the world is only the end of the world as you know it."
How like him, everyone thought. Then he was gone,
And the world was a blank. It was cold and the air was still.
Tell me, you people out there, what is poetry anyway?
        Can anyone die without even a little?

II

Our Masterpiece Is the Private Life

For Jules

I

Is THERE something down by the water keeping itself from us,
Some shy event, some secret of the light that falls upon the deep,
Some source of sorrow that does not wish to be discovered yet?

Why should we care? Doesn't desire cast its rainbows over the
    coarse porcelain
Of the world's skin and with its measures fill the air? Why look for
    more?

Our Masterpiece Is the Private Life

I I

AND NOW, while the advocates of awfulness and sorrow
Push their dripping barge up and down the beach, let's eat
Our brill, and sip this beautiful white Beaune.

True, the light is artificial, and we are not well-dressed.
So what. We like it here. We like the bullocks in the field next
    door,
We like the sound of wind passing over grass. The way you speak,

In that low voice, our late night disclosures . . . why live
For anything else? Our masterpiece is the private life.

Our Masterpiece Is the Private Life

III

STANDING on the quay between the Roving Swan and the Star
   Immaculate,
Breathing the night air as the moment of pleasure taken
In pleasure vanishing seems to grow, its self-soiling

Beauty, which can only be what it was, sustaining itself
A little longer in its going, I think of our own smooth passage
Through the graded partitions, the crises that bleed

Into the ordinary, leaving us a little more tired each time,
A little more distant from the experiences, which, in the old days,
Held us captive for hours. The drive along the winding road

Back to the house, the sea pounding against the cliffs,
The glass of whiskey on the table, the open book, the questions,
All the day's rewards waiting at the doors of sleep . . .

Morning, Noon, and Night

I

AND THE morning green, and the buildup of weather, and my brows
Have not been brushed, and never will be, by the breezes of divinity.
That much is clear, at least to me, but yesterday I noticed
Something floating in and out of clouds, something like a bird,
But also like a man, black-suited, with his arms outspread.
And I thought this could be a sign that I've been wrong. Then I woke,
And on my bed the shadow of the future fell, and on the liquid ruins
Of the sea outside, and on the shells of buildings at the water's edge.
A rapid overcast blew in, bending trees and flattening fields. I stayed
    in bed,
Hoping it would pass. What might have been still waited for its
    chance.

II

WHATEVER the star charts told us to watch for or the maps
Said we would find, nothing prepared us for what we discovered.
We toiled away in the shadowless depths of noon,
While an alien wind slept in the branches, and dead leaves
Turned to dust in the streets. Cities of light, long summers
Of leisure were not to be ours; for to come as we had, long after
It mattered, to live among tombs, great as they are,
Was to be no nearer the end, no farther from where we began.

Morning, Noon, and Night

III

THESE NIGHTS of pinks and purples vanishing, of freakish heat
That strokes our skin until we fall asleep and stray to places
We hoped would always be beyond our reach—the deeps
Where nothing flourishes, where everything that happens seems
To be for keeps. We sweat, and plead to be released
Into the coming day on time, and panic at the thought
Of never getting there and being forced to drift forgotten
On a midnight sea where every thousand years a ship is sighted, or
    a swan,
Or a drowned swimmer whose imagination has outlived his fate,
    and who swims
To prove, to no one in particular, how false his life had been.

A Piece of the Storm

For Sharon Horvath

FROM THE shadow of domes in the city of domes,
A snowflake, a blizzard of one, weightless, entered your room
And made its way to the arm of the chair where you, looking up
From your book, saw it the moment it landed. That's all
There was to it. No more than a solemn waking
To brevity, to the lifting and falling away of attention, swiftly,
A time between times, a flowerless funeral. No more than that
Except for the feeling that this piece of the storm,
Which turned into nothing before your eyes, would come back,
That someone years hence, sitting as you are now, might say:
"It's time. The air is ready. The sky has an opening."

A Suite of Appearances

To Octavio and Marie Jo Paz

I

OUT OF what dark or lack has he come to wait
At the edge of your gaze for the moment when you
Would look up and see through the trembling leaves

His shadow suddenly there? Out of what place has he come
To enter the light that remains, and say in the weightless
Cadence of those who arrive from a distance that the crossing

Was hard with only a gleam to follow over the Sea of Something,
Which opens and closes, breaks and flashes, spreading its cold,
Watery foliage wherever it can to catch you and carry you

And leave you where you have never been, that he has escaped
To tell you with all that is left of his voice that this is his
Story, which continues wherever the end is happening?

A Suite of Appearances

II

No WONDER—since things come into view then drop from
  sight—
We clear a space for ourselves, a stillness where nothing
Is blurred: a common palm, an oasis in which to rest, to sit

For hours beside the pool while the moonlight builds its palaces,
And columns rise, and coral chambers open onto patios
With songbirds practicing their peeps and trills.

No wonder the evening paper lies unread, no wonder what
  happened
Before tonight, the history of ourselves, leaves us cold.

A Suite of Appearances

III

How IT COMES forward, and deposits itself like wind
In the ear which hears only the humming at first, the first
Suggestion of what is to come, how it grows out of itself,

Out of the humming because if it didn't it would die
In the graveyard of sound without being known, and then
Nothing would happen for days or weeks until something like it

Came back, a sound announcing itself as your own, a voice
That is yours, bending under the weight of desire,
Suddenly turning your language into a field unfolding

And all the while the humming can still be detected, the original
Humming before it was yours, and you lie back and hear it,
Surprised that what you are saying was something you meant,

And you think that perhaps you are not who you thought, that
    henceforth
Any idea of yourself must include a body surrounding a song.

A Suite of Appearances

IV

IN ANOTHER time, we will want to know how the earth looked
Then, and were people the way we are now. In another time,
The records they left will convince us that we are unchanged

And could be at ease in the past, and not alone in the present.
And we shall be pleased. But beyond all that, what cannot
Be seen or explained will always be elsewhere, always supposed,

Invisible even beneath the signs—the beautiful surface,
The uncommon knowledge—that point its way. In another time,
What cannot be seen will define us, and we shall be prompted

To say that language is error, and all things are wronged
By representation. The self, we shall say, can never be
Seen with a disguise, and never be seen without one.

A Suite of Appearances

V

To SIT IN this chair and wonder where is endlessness
Born, where does it go, how close has it come; and to see
The snow coming down, the flakes enlarging whatever they touch,

Changing shapes until no shape remains. In their descent
They are like stars overtaken by light, or like thoughts
That drift before the long, blanks windows facing the future,

Withering, whirling, continuing down, finally away
From the clear panes into the place where nothing will do,
Where nothing is needed or said because it is already known.

And when it is over, and the deep, unspeakable reaches of white
Melt into memory, how will the warmth of the fire,
So long in coming, keep us from mourning the loss?

A Suite of Appearances

VI

Of occasions flounced with rose and gold in which the sun
Sinks deep and drowns in a blackening sea, of those, and more,
To be tired. To have the whole sunset again, moment by moment,

As it occurred, in a correct and detailed account, only darkens
Our sense of what happened. There is a limit to what we can picture
And to how much of a good thing is a good thing. Better to hope

For the merest reminder, a spectral glimpse—there but not there,
Something not quite a scene, poised only to be dissolved,
So, when it goes as it must, no sense of loss springs in its wake.

The houses, the gardens, the roaming dogs, let them become
The factors of absence, an incantation of the ineffable.
The backyard was red, that much we know. And the church bell

Tolled the hour. What more is there? The odors of food,
The last traces of dinner, are gone. The glasses are washed.
The neighborhood sleeps. Will the same day ever come back, and
    with it

Our amazement at having been in it, or will only a dark haze
Spread at the back of the mind, erasing events, one after
The other, so brief they may have been lost to begin with?

Here

THE SUN that silvers all the buildings here
Has slid behind a cloud, and left the once bright air
Something less than blue. Yet everything is clear.
Across the road, some dead plants dangle down from rooms
Unoccupied for months, two empty streets converge
On a central square, and on a nearby hill some tombs,
Half buried in a drift of wild grass, appear to merge
With houses at the edge of town. A breeze
Stirs up some dust, turns up a page or two, then dies.
All the boulevards are lined with leafless trees.
There are no dogs nosing around, no birds, no buzzing flies.
Dust gathers everywhere—on stools and bottles in the bars,
On shelves and racks of clothing in department stores,
On the blistered dashboards of abandoned cars.
Within the church, whose massive, rotting doors
Stay open, it is cool, so if a visitor should wander in
He could easily relax, kneel and pray,
Or watch the dirty light pour through the baldachin,
Or think about the heat outside that does not go away,
Which might be why there are no people there—who knows—
Or about the dragon that he saw when he arrived,
Curled up before its cave in saurian repose,
And about how good it is to be survived.

Two de Chiricos

For Harry Ford

1. *The Philosopher's Conquest*

THIS MELANCHOLY moment will remain,
So, too, the oracle beyond the gate,
And always the tower, the boat, the distant train.

Somewhere to the south a Duke is slain,
A war is won. Here, it is too late.
This melancholy moment will remain.

Here, an autumn evening without rain,
Two artichokes abandoned on a crate,
And always the tower, the boat, the distant train.

Is this another scene of childhood pain?
Why do the clockhands say 1:28?
This melancholy moment will remain.

The green and yellow light of love's domain
Falls upon the joylessness of fate,
And always the tower, the boat, the distant train.

The things our vision wills us to contain,
The life of objects, their unbearable weight.
This melancholy moment will remain,
And always the tower, the boat, the distant train.

Two de Chiricos

2. *The Disquieting Muses*

BOREDOM sets in first, and then despair.
One tries to brush it off. It only grows.
Something about the silence of the square.

Something is wrong; something about the air,
Its color; about the light, the way it glows.
Boredom sets in first, and then despair.

The muses in their fluted evening wear,
Their faces blank, might lead one to suppose
Something about the silence of the square,

Something about the buildings standing there.
But no, they have no purpose but to pose.
Boredom sets in first, and then despair.

What happens after that, one doesn't care.
What brought one here—the desire to compose
Something about the silence of the square,

Or something else, of which one's not aware,
Life itself, perhaps—who really knows?
Boredom sets in first, and then despair . . .
Something about the silence of the square.

Some Last Words

1

It is easier for a needle to pass through a camel
Than for a poor man to enter a woman of means.
Just go to the graveyard and ask around.

2

Eventually, you slip outside, letting the door
Bang shut on your latest thought. What was it anyway?
Just go to the graveyard and ask around.

3

"Negligence" is the perfume I love.
O Fedora. Fedora. If you want any,
Just go to the graveyard and ask around.

4

The bones of the buffalo, the rabbit at sunset,
The wind and its double, the tree, the town . . .
Just go to the graveyard and ask around.

Some Last Words

5

If you think good things are on their way
And the world will improve, don't hold your breath.
Just go to the graveyard and ask around.

6

You over there, why do you ask if this is the valley
Of limitless blue, and if we are its prisoners?
Just go to the graveyard and ask around.

7

Life is a dream that is never recalled when the sleeper awakes.
If this is beyond you, Magnificent One,
Just go to the graveyard and ask around.

III

Five Dogs

I

I, THE DOG they call Spot, was about to sing. Autumn
Had come, the walks were freckled with leaves, and a tarnished
Moonlit emptiness crept over the valley floor.
I wanted to climb the poets' hill before the winter settled in;
I wanted to praise the soul. My neighbor told me
Not to waste my time. Already the frost had deepened
And the north wind, trailing the whip of its own scream,
Pressed against the house. "A dog's sublimity is never news,"
He said, "what's another poet in the end?"
And I stood in the midnight valley, watching the great starfields
Flash and flower in the wished-for reaches of heaven.
That's when I, the dog they call Spot, began to sing.

Five Dogs

2

Now THAT the great dog I worshipped for years
Has become none other than myself, I can look within
And bark, and I can look at the mountains down the street
And bark at them as well. I am an eye that sees itself
Look back, a nose that tracks the scent of shadows
As they fall, an ear that picks up sounds
Before they're born. I am the last of the platinum
Retrievers, the end of a gorgeous line.
But there's no comfort being who I am.
I roam around and ponder fate's abolishments
Until my eyes are filled with tears and I say to myself, "Oh Rex,
Forget. Forget. The stars are out. The marble moon slides by."

Five Dogs

For Neil Welliver

3

MOST OF my kind believe that Earth
Is the only planet not covered with hair. So be it,
I say, let tragedy strike, let the story of everything
End today, then let it begin again tomorrow. I no longer care.
I no longer wait in front of the blistered, antique mirror,
Hoping a shape or a self will rise, and step
From that misted surface and say: You there,
Come with me into the world of light and be whole,
For the love you thought had been dead a thousand years
Is back in town and asking for you. Oh no.
I say, I'm done with my kind. I live alone
On Walnut Lane, and will until the day I die.

Five Dogs

(*After a line of John Ashbery's*)

4

BEFORE the tremendous dogs are unleashed,
Let's get the little ones inside, let's drag
The big bones onto the lawn and clean The Royal Dog Hotel.
Gypsy, my love, the end of an age has come. Already,
The howls of the great dogs practicing fills the air,
And look at that man on all fours dancing under
The moon's dumbfounded gaze, and look at that woman
Doing the same. The wave of the future has gotten
To them and they have responded with all they have:
A little step forward, a little step back. And they sway,
And their eyes are closed. O heavenly bodies.
O bodies of time. O golden bodies of lasting fire.

Five Dogs

5

ALL WINTER the weather came up with amazing results:
The streets and walks had turned to glass. The sky
Was a sheet of white. And here was a dog in a phone booth
Calling home. But nothing would ease his tiny heart.
For years the song of his body was all of his calling. Now
It was nothing. Those hymns to desire, songs of bliss
Would never return. The sky's copious indigo,
The yellow dust of sunlight after rain, were gone.
No one was home. The phone kept ringing. The curtains
Of sleep were about to be drawn, and darkness would pass
Into the world. And so, and so . . . goodbye all, goodbye dog.

IV

In Memory of Joseph Brodsky

IT COULD BE SAID, even here, that what remains of the self
Unwinds into a vanishing light, and thins like dust, and heads
To a place where knowing and nothing pass into each other, and
    through;
That it moves, unwinding still, beyond the vault of brightness ended,
And continues to a place which may never be found, where the
    unsayable,
Finally, once more is uttered, but lightly, quickly, like random rain
That passes in sleep, that one imagines passes in sleep.
What remains of the self unwinds and unwinds, for none
Of the boundaries holds—neither the shapeless one between us,
Nor the one that falls between your body and your voice. Joseph,
Dear Joseph, those sudden reminders of your having been—the
    places
And times whose greatest life was the one you gave them—now
    appear
Like ghosts in your wake. What remains of the self unwinds
Beyond us, for whom time is only a measure of meanwhile
And the future no more than et cetera et cetera . . . but fast and
    forever.

What It Was

I

IT WAS impossible to imagine, impossible
Not to imagine; the blueness of it, the shadow it cast,
Falling downward, filling the dark with the chill of itself,
The cold of it falling out of itself, out of whatever idea
Of itself it described as it fell; a something, a smallness,
A dot, a speck, a speck within a speck, an endless depth
Of smallness; a song, but less than a song, something drowning
Into itself, something going, a flood of sound, but less
Than a sound; the last of it, the blank of it,
The tender small blank of it filling its echo, and falling,
And rising unnoticed, and falling again, and always thus,
And always because, and only because, once having been, it was . . .

What It Was

I I

IT WAS the beginning of a chair;
It was the gray couch; it was the walls,
The garden, the gravel road; it was the way
The ruined moonlight fell across her hair.
It was that, and it was more. It was the wind that tore
At the trees; it was the fuss and clutter of clouds, the shore
Littered with stars. It was the hour which seemed to say
That if you knew what time it really was, you would not
Ask for anything again. It was that. It was certainly that.
It was also what never happened—a moment so full
That when it went, as it had to, no grief was large enough
To contain it. It was the room that appeared unchanged
After so many years. It was that. It was the hat
She'd forgotten to take, the pen she left on the table.
It was the sun on my hand. It was the sun's heat. It was the way
I sat, the way I waited for hours, for days. It was that. Just that.

The Delirium Waltz

I cannot remember when it began. The lights were low. We were walking across the floor, over polished wood and inlaid marble, through shallow water, through dustings of snow, through cloudy figures of fallen light. I cannot remember but I think you were there—whoever you were—sometimes with me, sometimes watching. Shapes assembled themselves and dissolved. The hall to the ballroom seemed endless, and a voice—perhaps it was yours—was saying we'd never arrive. Now we were gliding over the floor, our clothes were heavy, the music was slow, and I thought we would die all over again. I believe we were happy. We moved in the drift of sound, and whether we went towards the future or back to the past we weren't able to tell. Anxiety has its inflections—wasteful, sad, tragic at times—but here it had none. In its harmless hovering it was merely fantastic, so we kept dancing. I think I was leading. Why else would I practice those near calamitous dips? I think it was clear that we had always been dancing, always been eager to give ourselves to the rapture music of. Even the simplest movement, from the wafting of clouds to the wink of an eye, could catch and hold our attention. The rooms became larger and finally dimensionless, and we kept gliding, gliding and turning.

The Delirium Waltz

And then came Bob and Sonia
And the dance was slow
And joining them now were Chip and Molly
And Joseph dear Joseph was dancing and smoking

And the dance was slow
And into the hall years later came Tom and Em
And Joseph dear Joseph was dancing and smoking
And Bill and Sandy were leaning together

And into the hall years later came Tom and Em
Holding each other and turning and turning
And Bill and Sandy were leaning together
And Wally and Deb and Jorie and Jim

Holding each other and turning and turning
Then came Jules tall and thin
And Wally and Deb and Jorie and Jim
Everyone moving everyone dancing

The Delirium Waltz

Then came Jules tall and thin
Across the wide floor
Everyone moving everyone dancing
Harry was there and so was Kathleen

Across the wide floor
Looking better than ever came Jessie and Steve
Harry was there and so was Kathleen
And Peter and Barbara had just gotten back

Looking better than ever came Jessie and Steve
Leon and Judith Muffie and Jim
And Peter and Barbara had just gotten back
And others were there

Leon and Judith Muffie and Jim
Charlie and Helen were eating and dancing
And others were there
Wearing their best

Charlie and Helen were eating and dancing
Glenn and Angela Buck and Cathy
Wearing their best
Around and around dancing and dancing

The Delirium Waltz

And our shadows floated away towards sunset and darkened the backs of birds, and blackened the sea whose breath smelled slightly of fish, of almonds, of rotting fruit. Soon the air was soiled with dust and purple clouds. We were standing, watching everyone else afloat on the floor, on the sea of the floor, like a raft of voices. "Hello," they said, as they sailed by, "may we have this dance?" And off they went to another room with pale blue walls and birds.

And one room led to another
And birds flew back and forth
People roamed the veranda
Under the limbs of trees

And birds flew back and forth
A golden haze was everywhere
Under the limbs of trees
And Howie was there with Francine

A golden haze was everywhere
And Jeannette and Buddy were dancing
And Howie was there with Francine
Angels must always be pale they said

The Delirium Waltz

And Jeannette and Buddy were dancing
And Louise and Karen were talking
Angels must always be pale they said
But pale turns round to white

And Louise and Karen were talking
Saying that blue slides into black
But pale turns round to white
And Jules was there in heels

Saying that blue slides into black
Rosanna was there and Maria
And Jules was there in heels
And day and night were one

Rosanna was there and Maria
And Rusty and Carol were there
And day and night were one
And the sea's green body was near

The Delirium Waltz

And Rusty and Carol were there
And Charles and Holly were dancing
And the sea's green body was near
Hello out there hello

And Charles and Holly were dancing
So thin they were and light
Hello out there hello
Can anyone hear out there

And the rush of water was loud as if the ballroom were flooded. And
I was dancing alone in the absence of all that I knew and was bound
by. And here was the sea—the blur, the erasure of difference, the
end of self, the end of whatever surrounds the self. And I kept going.
The breakers flashed and fell under the moon's gaze. Scattered
petals of foam shone briefly, then sank in the sand. It was cold, and
I found myself suddenly back with the others. That vast ungraspable
body, the sea, that huge and meaningless empire of water, was left
on its own.

The Delirium Waltz

They drifted over the floor
And the silver sparkled a little
Oh how they moved together
The crystals shook in the draft

And the silver sparkled a little
So many doors were open
The crystals shook in the draft
Nobody knew what would happen

So many doors were open
And there was Eleanor dancing
Nobody knew what would happen
Now Red waltzed into the room

And there was Eleanor dancing
And Don and Jean were waiting
Now Red waltzed into the room
The years would come and go

The Delirium Waltz

And Don and Jean were waiting
Hours and hours would pass
The years would come and go
The palms in the hallway rustled

Hours and hours would pass
Now enter the children of Em
The palms in the hallway rustled
And here were the children of Tom

Now enter the children of Em
There was nothing to do but dance
And here were the children of Tom
And Nolan was telling them something

There was nothing to do but dance
They would never sit down together
And Nolan was telling them something
And many who wished they could

The Delirium Waltz

Would never sit down together
The season of dancing was endless
And many who wished they could
Would never be able to stop

I cannot remember when it began. The lights were low. We were
walking across the floor, over polished wood and inlaid marble,
through shallow water, through dustings of snow, through cloudy
figures of fallen light. I cannot remember, but I think you were
there, whoever you were.

The View

For Derek Walcott

THIS IS the place. The chairs are white. The table shines.
The person sitting there stares at the waxen glow.
The wind moves the air around, repeatedly,
As if to clear a space. "A space for me," he thinks.
He's always been drawn to the weather of leavetaking,
Arranging itself so that grief—even the most intimate—
Might be read from a distance. A long shelf of cloud
Hangs above the open sea with the sun, the sun
Of no distinction, sinking behind it—a mild version
Of the story that is told just once if true, and always too late.
The waitress brings his drink, which he holds
Against the waning light, but just for a moment.
Its red reflection tints his shirt. Slowly the sky becomes darker,
The wind relents, the view sublimes. The violet sweep of it
Seems, in this effortless nightfall, more than a reason
For being there, for seeing it, seems itself a kind
Of happiness, as if that plain fact were enough and would last.

A Note About the Author

Mark Strand was born in Summerside, Prince Edward Island, Canada, and was raised and educated in the United States. He is the author of eight earlier books of poems. He is also the author of a book of stories, *Mr. and Mrs. Baby*, several volumes of translations (Rafael Alberti and Carlos Drummond de Andrade among them), a number of anthologies (most recently *100 Great Poems of the Twentieth Century*) and monographs on the contemporary artists William Bailey and Edward Hopper. He has received many honors and grants for his poems, including a MacArthur Fellowship, and in 1990 he was chosen as Poet Laureate of the United States. In 1993, he was awarded the Bollingen Prize, and in 1999, he was awarded the Pulitzer Prize in poetry for *Blizzard of One*. He lives in New York and teaches at Columbia University.

A Note About the Type

This book was set in a computer version of linotype Janson, a recutting made direct from type cast from matrices long thought to have been made by the Dutchman Anton Janson, a type founder in Leipzig (1668–1687). However, it has been conclusively demonstrated that the types are the work of Nicholas Kis (1650–1702), a Hungarian, who probably learned his trade from the Dutch type founder Dirk Voskens.

Composition by NK Graphics, Keene, New Hampshire
Printed by The Stinehour Press, Lunenburg, Vermont
Bound by Quebecor Printing, Brattleboro, Vermont
Designed by Harry Ford

Printed in the United States
by Baker & Taylor Publisher Services